To

From

P9-DLZ-293

Other books in this series:
HAPPY ANNIVERSARY
To a very special BROTHER
To a very special DAD
To a very special DAUGHTER
To a very special FRIEND
To a very special GRANDDAUGHTER
To a very special GRANDMA
To a very special GRANDPA
To a very special GRANDSON
Wishing you HAPPINESS

To my very special HUSBAND
Someone very special...
    TO THE ONE I LOVE
To a very special MOTHER
To a very special SISTER
To a very special SON
Wishing you happiness
    FOR YOUR WEDDING
To my very special WIFE

Published in 1995 by Helen Exley Giftbooks in Great Britain.
This edition published in 2008

12 11 10 9 8 7 6 5 4 3 2 1

ISBN 13: 978-1-84634-294-3

Helen Exley Giftbooks, 16 Chalk Hill, Watford, Herts WD19 4BG, UK.
www.helenexleygiftbooks.com

To a very special®
TEACHER

ILLUSTRATIONS BY JULIETTE CLARKE.
WRITTEN BY PAM BROWN.
EDITED BY HELEN EXLEY.

Thank you for making school
a place we love to go to in the morning.

HELEN EXLEY®

THANK YOU FOR EVERYTHING

Thank you for making learning not a job but a joy.

Thank you for making me feel valuable.

Thank you for helping me to discover
what I do best – and to do it even better.

Thank you for untangling tangles.

Thank you for taking away the fear of things
I could not understand – and persuading me
that I understood them after all.

Thank you for being someone
I can always trust
– and turn to when life gets difficult.

Some teachers make passing exams and getting
good grades the only reason for learning.
Thank you for showing us that it can be fun.

Thank you for persuading me that I was better
than I suspected.

Thank you for never seeing mistakes as failures
but as ways to learn.

It's as hard to be clever as to be a little slow.
Thank you for understanding all of us
and giving us the time and care each of us needs.

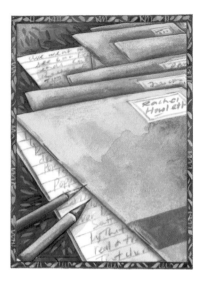

You never
make us feel you
are just stuffing us
with facts.
Instead –
you go *with* us
on voyages
of discovery.

OPENING DOORS FOR US

You have taught us to have adventures in our heads
– to search and discover, to live with amazement.

Good teachers can persuade their students
that learning is not an imposition, an interference,
a theft of freedom – but an excitement, and the key
to a greater freedom than they have ever known.

When you told us about the wise and the good
and the clever, the thinkers and makers and
dreamers – people who changed the world
– you always reminded us that they
were children once and had everything to learn.
It gave us the heart to try.

A class and a teacher who have
just defeated a difficult problem beam at
each other in delight.

A good teacher takes the everyday things of life,
the things a child knows,
and fashions them into stepping stones
of knowledge and growth.

A class bewitched by a problem,
a discovery, an experience, fizzes like a firework
and celebrates in stars!

WHAT KINDNESS MEANS

When every detail of what you taught
has been forgotten, a touch of
your enthusiasm, encouragement and
kindness will remain.

Thank you for never being sarcastic
– that's the thing that baffles and
bewilders a child.

A good teacher gives the best job
– like feeding the tadpoles, watering
the plants, or looking after the little ones
– to the saddest person.

A good teacher remembers being small
– and understands the terrors and
the sadnesses, the excitements and
the joys of the children in the class.

A good teacher knows when you
are very sad. Even if you haven't
said anything at all. And lets
you know you can tell her all about it.
If you want to.

All teachers are busy. There's always far too
much for any human to do. But, when
you're really low, your teacher has the time.

LESSONS IN LIFE

Become good at anything
and you will love life more.
That's what you said.
And it's true.

A good teacher can help us
make something of our lives,
however bad times are.

People often hurt other people
because they don't
understand what it feels like.

You made us feel at ease
and realize truths like these.

Thank you for showing us that we can learn from
failure, discover strength in difficulties,
find love and kindness in our darkest days.
Thank you for giving us the courage to use our
minds as well and as honestly as we can...
and never be afraid to question.
Thank you for showing us how to stand firm for
what we believe right... even when we are
shaking in our shoes.

You made us feel it is perfectly all right
to be ordinary – because ordinary people aren't
really ordinary at all. Each one has something
special they can do. And every one ⸻
valuable to the people that they lov
But, if you don't want to be ordinary,
you needn't ⸍⸍. Who knows what you can do
if you follow your special beliefs with all
mind and courage.

A CLASSROOM THAT IS SAFE

A classroom can simply be an extension of
the threatening world – or it can be an oasis.
Whatever chaos reigned outside – we knew we'd
find order, justice and a chance to learn
inside your classroom. And tolerance.
And laughter. And excitement.

Images of violence, anger and of greed
engulf us. But in our class we felt safe.
In this small space we learned to value
one another, to think, to learn, to wonder,
to find peace and create.
The ugliness and the greed of the world
was kept away long enough
for us to gather strength to stand against them.
You have shown us the value of kindness.
You have shown us the power of patience,
of courage, of dedication.

HAPPY, LEARNING, ACHIEVING

One Monday you said,

"*Now* I understand. You explained that very well."

One Tuesday you said,

"Great Heavens – that is beautiful. How did you
get that luminous effect...?"

One Wednesday you said,

"Could you make a copy of your poem for me to keep?'

One Thursday you said,

"Come out in front and show the class."

One Friday you said,

"Thank you. That was very, very kind."

And so gave five children gifts to last a lifetime.

You never pushed us up an unexplored rockface –
whether it was geography, history,
computer studies, algebra or poetry.
Or real granite. You showed us the holds.
You carefully guided us and made us feel
absolutely safe.

A good teacher gives you words, images,
ideas from which to build your life.
Whatever I build,
you helped to lay the foundations

There's a sort of buzz in a happy, learning
classroom. And we had it.

I LIKE TEACHERS...
who write clearly on the board,
who admit when they've made a mistake,
who read stories with lots of
different voices,
who don't mind when you sing off key –
just so long as you are enjoying
the singing,
who would rather be a little ordinary
than always bossy and powerful,
who smile a lot,
who have little catch-phrases like
"lots of hush now please" or
"all I want to hear now is the
swoosh of pencils."

I like teachers who understand when I don't understand. And explain things clearly. And notice when I put my hand up. And listen quietly to my problems.

And give me a turn at feeding the hamster. And smile when I've tried hard. And cheer and clap when our play is over. And tell us interesting things and give us interesting things to do.

I like teachers who don't mind going over their explanations again. And again. And again.

POOR TEACHER! POOR YOU!

I think there are words that will strike ice
into all teachers' hearts:

"My dad says you are wrong because..."

"Emily's swallowed a button..."

"My arm has gone all spotty."

"My grandma wants to visit you
about my reading."

Ordinary people have nightmares about
crocodiles or getting lost.
But I think teachers must have nightmares about
indignant, shouting parents.
And that William or Maya has dropped coffee
on their homework again.

Teachers do not wake in the night from
a dream of pursuing wolves, wild-eyed
and desperate. They dream they have left
all the school projects on a bus.

Some poor teachers are expected to deal
with children that have defeated
their parents, their doctor, a psychiatrist,
or two, and a gaggle of social workers.
They are usually told that all that's needed is
a Normal Classroom Environment.

A GOOD TEACHER…

Fairness, honesty, perseverance.

These are the legacy, the gift of a good teacher.

A good teacher can change your world.

A good teacher notices when a child is trying
– even if the results are minute.

A good teacher sees that everyone gets a turn
at the interesting jobs – and at the grotty ones.

Great careers can often be traced back to the
influence of one teacher.

A good teacher knows a word of praise
can give encouragement on the gloomiest day.

A good teacher can look at a page of writing
that looks like tangled knitting
and figure out
what you're trying to say.
She doesn't rewrite it.
She just gives it a sort of shake
– and it all falls into place.

A good teacher is as pleased as you are
when, at last, you succeed.

You will hear yourself
repeating your teacher's words, for decades.

ALWAYS GUIDING, ALWAYS ENCOURAGING

You make learning an adventure –
instead of a forced march.
You take us a step at a time, at a speed
that suits us. And if some of us discover
we can move forward in leaps –
you are delighted. And if some of us
plod happily along –
that gives you equal pleasure.

And you're most excited when
the weakest of us find our feet and begin to
catch up with the others.

A good teacher does not
impatiently shove you – and does not mutter
or grumble or nag from behind.

A good teacher walks beside you –
lets you explore, invent, create, question, explain.
With a hand ready to steady you
when you're really stuck.

A good teacher says "Look." "Think." "Try."
"What would happen if
we tried it the other way round?"
"Show me how to do it."

VALUES FOR LIFE

You told us that to do a little thing well is better than doing a large thing badly.

You taught us that excellence costs. Everyone has to decide just how much they are prepared to pay.

Thank you for making us value the differences
between each other instead of fearing them.

A good teacher shows you how much you
can do on your own – and how much more
you can do working with others.

You taught us that if we want to do something
very much, and work at it, and enjoy it and
become better at it – then it doesn't
much matter if we become famous or not.

You assured us that the great scientist and
the great artist were once as little as we are
and made mistakes and got confused.

You were the one who made me realize
that a life can be as thin and flat
as paper – or deep
as the ocean. We have to choose.

I WILL REMEMBER

You had a way with things.
The class will never forget you.
Neither will I.

School is a trial run for the world and a
teacher can only do so much to
help us through it. But teachers try.
They do their best.
And better than their best.

And we, free to leave, say goodbye
and walk off with a mixture of regret and a
strange excitement about new chapters in
our lives. We know that you have given us
something that will be part of us forever.

Teachers are remembered more for what they
were than what they taught.

I will remember you always and always.